Barn Owls

Nocturnal Hunters

Rebecca Rissman

Heinemann
LIBRARY

Chicago, Illinois

Edited by Brynn Baker, Clare Lewis, and Helen Cox Cannons
Designed by Kyle Grenz and Tim Bond
Picture research by Tracy Cummins
Production by Helen McCreath
Originated by Capstone Global Library Ltd

Library of Congress Cataloging-in-Publication Data

ISBN 978-1-4846-0310-9 (hardcover)
ISBN 978-1-4846-0316-1 (paperback)
ISBN 978-1-4846-0328-4 (ebook PDF)

Acknowledgments

We would like to thank the following for permission to reproduce photographs:FLPA: Derek Middleton, 7 mouse, Erica Olsen, 19, Gary K Smith, 21, Imagebroker, 5, 23d, Michael Durham/Minden Pictures, 7 bat, Paul Sawer, 17, Simon Litten, 20, 23c; Getty Images: Derrick Hamrick, 1, 23g, Oxford Scientific/Michael Leach, front cover; Science Source: Kenneth M. Highfill, 9; Shutterstock: Andrew Astbury, 7 fox, CreativeNature.nl, 10, Dr. Morley Read, 14, 15, 23e, Gerckens-Photo-Hamburg, 18, 23f, iceeyes198369, 6, Mark Bridger, 4, 23a, back cover, Miles Away Photography, 22, Stephen Mcsweeny, 12, Tom Reichner, 11, Piotr Krzeslak, 7 hedgehog; Superstock: imagebroker.net, 16, 23b

Every effort has been made to contact copyright holders of material reproduced in this book. Any omissions will be rectified in subsequent printings if notice is given to the publisher.

All the Internet addresses (URLs) given in this book were valid at the time of going to press. However, due to the dynamic nature of the Internet, some addresses may have changed, or sites may have changed or ceased to exist since publication. While the author and publisher regret any inconvenience this may cause readers, no responsibility for any such changes can be accepted by either the author or the publisher.

Contents

What Is a Barn Owl?

A barn owl is a large bird. Its body is covered in gray or brown feathers.

It has light-colored feathers on its face.

A barn owl has sharp claws called talons. It has large eyes and a strong **beak**.

You rarely see barn owls during the day because they are **nocturnal**.

What Does Nocturnal Mean?

Animals that are nocturnal are awake at night.

Nocturnal animals sleep during the day.

bat

fox

hedgehog

mouse

Many animals are nocturnal.

Bats, foxes, hedgehogs, and mice are nocturnal.

7

Where Do Barn Owls Live?

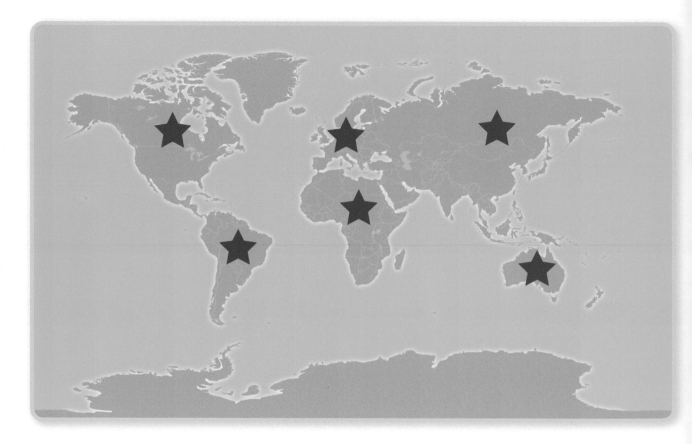

Barn owls live in Europe, North America, South America, Africa, Asia, and Australia.

They can live in forests, fields, deserts, farmlands, and even in cities.

Barn owls make nests in trees, caves, and buildings.

They are called barn owls because they often make nests in barns.

What Do Barn Owls Eat?

Barn owls hunt for nocturnal animals.

They usually eat small animals, such as mice and bats.

Some barn owls even eat larger animals, such as baby rabbits.

Barn owls also eat other small birds.

How Do Barn Owls Find Prey?

Barn owls have very good hearing. They listen for **prey**.

Barn owls also have good eyesight. They can see small animals moving in the dark.

Barn owls fly quietly after prey.
They catch prey with their sharp talons.

What Are Owl Pellets?

Owls often swallow their prey whole.

After they eat, they spit out **pellets**.

Pellets are the bones, fur, and feathers of owl prey.

Pellets show the different animals an owl has eaten.

What Are Baby Barn Owls Like?

Female barn owls lay eggs in springtime.

Owl chicks are covered in **down** shortly after they hatch.

The mother owl brings prey back to the nest to feed the chicks.

Young owls leave the nest after two months.

Do Barn Owls Have Predators?

Barn owls have few **predators**.

In some places, raccoons, cats, and larger owls eat barn owl chicks.

Humans can harm barn owls too.

Growing cities and new buildings can make it hard for barn owls to find enough prey to eat.

How Can You Spot Barn Owls?

Barn owls are easiest to spot at **dusk**.
Watch for them swooping low over fields.

Owl droppings and pellets can tell you that a nest is nearby.

Listen for barn owl screeches. They can sometimes tell you where a nest is.

Barn Owl Body Map

wing

beak

talon

Picture Glossary

 **beak** a bird's hard jaw

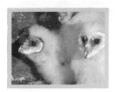 **down** soft, fluffy feathers of a young bird

 **dusk** time of day when the sun sets

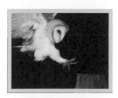 **nocturnal** awake at night and asleep during the day

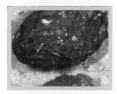 **pellet** bones, fur, and feathers of owl prey

 **predator** animal that hunts other animals for food

 **prey** animal that is hunted by other animals

Find Out More

Books

Bodden, Valerie. *Owls.* Amazing Animals. Mankato, Minn.: Creative Education, 2013.

Dunn, Mary R. *Owls.* Nocturnal Animals. Mankato, Minn.: Capstone Press, 2012.

Websites

Discover more about barn owls at:
http://allaboutbirds.org/guide/Barn_Owl/id

Learn more about owls at:
http://bbc.co.uk/nature/life/owl

Index

Nocturnal Hunters
Barn Owls

Where do barn owls live, and what do they eat?

When you want to find out...

Heinemann
Read and Learn

Read and Learn is an extensive collection of nonfiction books that helps young readers discover and understand the world around them. Headings in the form of questions help children to focus and ask their own questions. Each book contains a glossary and an index, offering young readers an introduction to these important features of nonfiction text.

About the author:
Rebecca Rissman has written more than 100 nonfiction books for children, including many books about animals and the natural world.

Book consultant:
Michael Bright has traveled all over the world to film animals and habitats for the BBC Natural History Unit. He has also written books about sharks and other animals.

Barn Owls   978-1-4846-0316-1
Bats   978-1-4846-0315-4
Hedgehogs   978-1-4846-0319-2
Mice   978-1-4846-0317-8
Red Foxes   978-1-4846-0318-5

Level: K

Heinemann Raintree

a capstone imprint   CapstoneClassroom.com

ISBN 978-1-4846-0316-1

90000

9 781484 603161